Being in Government

So You Want to Be a U. S. REPRESENTATIVE

by Kassandra Radomski

Consultant:
Fred Slocum,
Associate Professor of Political Science,
Minnesota State University, Mankato

CAPSTONE PRESS
a capstone imprint

Fact Finders Books are published by Capstone Press
1710 Roe Crest Drive, North Mankato, Minnesota 56003
www.mycapstone.com

Library of Congress Cataloging-in-Publication Data
Names: Radomski, Kassandra, author.
Title: So you want to be a U.S. representative / by Kassandra Radomski.
Other titles: So you want to be a US representative | So you want to be a
    United States representative
Description: North Mankato, Minnesota : Capstone Press, [2020] | Series: Fact Finders.
    Being in government | Audience: Ages: 8 to 9. | Audience: Grades: 4 to 6.
Identifiers: LCCN 2019004861| ISBN 9781543571967 (hardcover) | ISBN 9781543575286
    (paperback) | ISBN 9781543572001 (ebook PDF)
Subjects: LCSH: United States. Congress. House—Juvenile literature. | Legislators—United
States—Juvenile literature. | Vocational guidance—Juvenile literature.
Classification: LCC JK1319 .R325 2020 | DDC 328.73/072023—dc23
LC record available at https://lccn.loc.gov/2019004861

Editorial Credits
Mari Bolte, editor; Jennifer Bergstrom, designer;
Jo Miller, media researcher; Laura Manthe, production specialist

Image Credits
Newscom: CQ Roll Call/Bill Clark, 12, CQ Roll Call/Tom Williams, 19, 23, KRT/POOL, 20,
Polaris/CNP/Ron Sachs, 14, 27, REUTERS/Yuri Gripas, 24, Sipa USA/Abaca/Douliery
Olivier/Abaca Press, 29, Sipa USA/Cheriss May, 28, UPI Photo Service/Roger L. Wollenberg,
25, UPI/Kevin Dietsch, 9, UPI/Pat Benic, 17, ZUMA Press/Douglas Christian, 6, ZUMA
Press/Jim West, 16, Shutterstock: Cvandyke, 5, Everett Historical, 21, Hogan Imaging,
Cover, JPL Designs, 11; Wikimedia: United States Census 2010, modified by Adam Lenhardt,
modified by User:Philosopher, 8

Design Elements
Capstone; Shutterstock: advent, primiaou, Rebellion Works, simbos

Printed in the United States of America.
PA70

TABLE OF CONTENTS

WANTED:
U.S. REPRESENTATIVE

Do you like meeting new people? Is it your dream to help others solve their problems? Is working with others a strength? Are you a great fundraiser? Have you ever been curious about what a U.S. representative does? If you answered "yes" to any of these questions, then becoming a member of Congress may be for you!

Requirements for Being a U.S. Representative

There are three requirements for this job. Candidates must be:

✓ at least 25 years old

✓ U.S. citizens for at least seven years before being elected

✓ residents of the state they want to represent

The House of Representatives meets in the south wing of the United States Capitol Building. The Senate meets in the north wing.

High school and college degrees are not required for this job. However, they are strongly recommended.

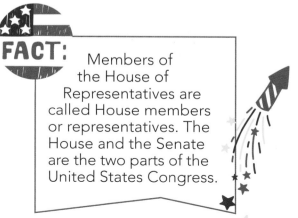

FACT: Members of the House of Representatives are called House members or representatives. The House and the Senate are the two parts of the United States Congress.

Hawaii Representative Tulsi Gabbard announced the first bill of the 116th Congress in February 2019.

Representatives make laws. They spend time talking to people in their home states and districts. They talk about the problems and issues those people face. Then they bring those concerns to the U.S. Capitol Building in Washington, D.C. Maybe a new law can fix things.

The House decides how the government will spend tax money. It also oversees the president and the president's **administration**. If a presidential race is tied, the House breaks that tie.

Ideal candidates must be willing to work long hours. Representatives often work 70 or more hours each week. That's much more than the typical 40 hours many full-time employees work! But they are paid well—a representative's salary is $174,000 a year. They also get excellent perks, such as health insurance and retirement benefits. An allowance for travel, office expenses, and staff is included too.

Representatives serve for two years. When their term is up, they can run for re-election. Some representatives are re-elected and serve for many years.

IN THE FAMILY

A member of the Dingell family has represented Michigan for nearly 90 years.

In 1955 U.S. Representative John Dingell Sr. died while still in office. He had been elected in 1933. His 29-year-old son John Dingell Jr. was chosen in a special election to complete his father's term. He was re-elected 28 times after that, serving until his retirement in 2014 at the age of 87. The longest-serving member of Congress, John passed away in 2019.

John's wife, Debbie, was elected to his U.S. House seat in 2014. She was re-elected in 2016 and 2018.

administration—the period of time during which a government holds office

How Many Are There?

There are 50 senators who serve in Congress. That's two per state. But there are a lot more representatives—435 of them! The number of representatives in each state depends on that state's population. Less populated states might only have one or two. More populated states have more. California has the most, with 53.

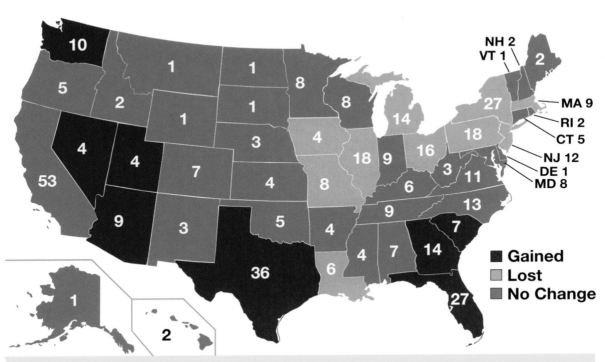

A map showing the distribution of representatives based on the 2010 census. The next census will be taken in 2020.

OTHER REPRESENTATIVES

Five U.S. territories (American Samoa, Guam, the Northern Mariana Islands, the U.S. Virgin Islands, and Puerto Rico) and the District of Columbia each have a delegate in the House of Representatives. These delegates can speak, offer amendments, and join and vote on House committees. However, they cannot vote on matters involving House legislation.

Delegates take their oaths and are sworn in with the rest of the representatives.

Most states are divided into two or more congressional districts. Most districts have around 710,000 people. In total, there are 435 districts across the country. Each gets a representative. The seven lowest-population states—Delaware, Vermont, Alaska, Montana, Wyoming, North Dakota, and South Dakota—are not divided into districts. In those states, the representative serves the entire state.

MAKING LAWS

The U.S. government is made up of three parts: the **legislative**, **judicial**, and **executive** branches. The legislative branch makes laws. The judicial branch interprets them. The executive branch carries them out. The House of Representatives and the Senate are part of the legislative branch.

Do you like to learn? Representatives spend a lot of time learning about concerns their **constituents** face. Sometimes those concerns become bills. Eventually, some of those bills become laws.

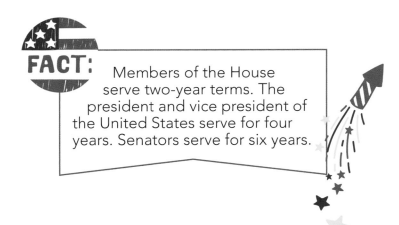

FACT: Members of the House serve two-year terms. The president and vice president of the United States serve for four years. Senators serve for six years.

★ THE ★
THREE BRANCHES OF GOVERNMENT

LEGISLATIVE
Makes Laws

EXECUTIVE
Carries Out Laws

JUDICIAL
Interprets Laws

Congress
House of Representatives
Senate

President
Vice President
Cabinet

Supreme Court
Other Federal Courts

CONSTITUTION
created the three branches

constituents—the people who live and vote in a Congress member's home state or district

executive branch—the part of government that makes sure the laws are obeyed

judicial branch—the part of government that explains laws

legislative branch—the part of government that passes bills that become laws

If a representative decides an issue is important, he or she may write a bill about it. The representative who introduces the bill on the House floor is called the bill's sponsor. The bill is put into a wooden box called a hopper. Then the work of turning a bill into law begins.

Bills may be seen by a single committee, or two or more committees. Sometimes they go to more than one committee at the same time. Other times, one committee might see the bill first. Then it will go to another. Assigning a bill to one or more committees or subcommittees is called referral.

Working groups that bring both Republican and Democratic representatives together to discuss issues relating to bills are called bipartisan.

★ HOW A ★
BILL IS MADE

representative introduces the bill on the House floor

bill is given a name that starts with HR (for House of Representatives) and a number*

bill is sent to one or more committees; representatives talk about the bill, research the issue, make changes, and then vote on whether to approve it

APPROVED

bill goes to the House floor**

if a majority agrees, bill goes to the Senate; senators discuss and then vote

bill may go to another committee or subcommittee

if a majority agrees, the bill goes to the president, who signs or vetoes

bill becomes a law

SIGNED

NOT APPROVED

a bill defeated in committee cannot be discussed or voted on until the next Congressional session; likely dead

VETOED

bill can still become law if at least 67 out of 100 senators and 290 out of 435 representatives override the veto

*bills starting in the Senate are named with an S
**the House, Senate, and president must agree on the exact same bill before it can be passed.

Issues relating to the bill are researched and discussed. Changes may be made. Subcommittees focus on how the bills apply to more narrow areas of policy.

Speaker of the House Nancy Pelosi accepts the Clerk's Gavel from outgoing Speaker Kevin McCarthy. Pelosi used the gavel to call the 116th Congress to order on January 3, 2019.

In Session

A new Congress begins at noon on January 3 during odd-numbered years. The representatives meet and the House is called to order. A prayer is offered, and then the Speaker of the House opens the session. The Speaker is the head of the **majority party** and the most powerful member of the House.

The Speaker announces any updates to the meeting program. He or she also approves the **minutes** of the meeting from the previous day. After that, a member of the House leads the Pledge of Allegiance. One-minute speeches follow. These speeches give representatives the chance to address the floor in 300 words or less. Sometimes a representative wants to clarify an opinion. Other times the speeches are not related to House business at all. Permission to talk is granted by the Speaker.

Then the House votes on bills. Those bills can vary in importance, length, and complexity, but they all must be voted on. Some votes are nonpolitical and are passed **unanimously**, such as renaming a federal highway or post office. Many other votes are political. Debating may take place. Bills that were not approved previously can be amended, discussed, and brought to the floor.

FACT: The House of Representatives schedule can be viewed online. You can see when it is in session and what was discussed each day.

majority party—the party whose members make up more than half of the total membership of the group

minutes—written notes that tell what took place at a meeting

unanimous—agreed on by everyone

You can find town hall meetings in your area online.

FACT: Representatives are busy! Sometimes their workdays are planned out in periods as short as 5 minutes. Photo opportunities, interviews, checking email, and reading the news are all part of a representative's day.

Dividing Their Time

Ready to hop on a plane and go? Grab your frequent flyer card! Most representatives divide their time between Washington, D.C., and their home district. At home they may attend events for important causes. They also spend a lot of time raising campaign money. Phone calls, door knocking, and personal meetings with potential donors are all ways to gain support and money. Longer-serving representatives are also expected to raise money for their political parties.

Meeting with constituents is important. Sometimes members of the public get together to hold town hall meetings. Representatives are strongly expected to attend these meetings. Town halls provide opportunities for constituents to ask questions or speak out about issues they care about.

Representatives spend the rest of their time in Washington while the House is in session. Sessions begin in early January of odd-numbered years. They break for recess in August of the next even-numbered year. The next session begins the January after the election in the even-numbered year.

AN EXPENSIVE JOB

Having two homes and two offices, one in the representative's home district and another in Washington, D.C., can get expensive. Representatives don't get an allowance for housing. Some members of Congress sleep in their offices or share apartments with other politicians to save money.

The House is in session about 138 days a year.

WHAT ELSE DO REPRESENTATIVES DO?

Are you good at handling money? The United States Constitution gives Congress the power to collect taxes and spend money. This is called the power of **appropriations**. Money collected through taxes helps to pay for government-supported activities and programs. Some of these include the military, the postal service, early childhood education programs, health care, veterans' benefits, science research, food assistance, and much more.

FACT: The power of representatives to levy taxes and spend the federal government's money is called the appropriations power, or the "power of the purse."

Representatives Kevin Brady (left) and Rich Neal prepare for a Senate-House committee meeting. Together they ran the Ways and Means Committee in 2017.

COMMITTEES

There are 20 committees within the House of Representatives. Each discusses relevant bills and issues. Committees include Armed Services; Agriculture; Education and Workforce; Ethics; Homeland Security; and Science, Space, and Technology. Committee members are recommended and assigned based on interests and current committee sizes.

appropriations—the congressional power to collect taxes and authorize spending federal government money

19

Other Duties

If a presidential election is tied, representatives decide the winner. This has happened three times in American history—in 1800, 1824, and 1876.

Representatives can also call for a president or judge's **impeachment**. They make a list of the official's alleged misdeeds. This document is called the Articles of Impeachment. Once the list is complete, the House votes on each article. A majority of the representatives—at least 218—must agree on at least one article for the impeachment to move forward.

Representative Henry Hyde read the Articles of Impeachment against President Bill Clinton in 1999.

IMPEACHMENT TRIAL
PRESENTATION OF ARTICLES

C-SPAN2
U.S. SENATE

SOMEONE HAS TO PICK

Aaron Burr
(1756–1836)

In 1800 the presidential race was tied between Thomas Jefferson and Aaron Burr. They had started as running mates under the Democratic-Republican party. Their opponents were John Adams and Charles C. Pinckney of the Federalist party. Together, though, Jefferson and Burr won the most electoral votes. At the time, whoever won the most electoral votes became president, even if one person on the ticket ran as the vice presidential candidate.

The House of Representatives now had to choose which candidate would become the president. In the end, 10 states voted for Jefferson and four for Burr. In 1804 the Constitution was amended to say that candidates running together must run for either president or vice president.

If the House votes for impeachment, the Senate decides whether or not the official should be removed from office. A two-thirds majority vote is required.

For federal officials, their punishment may not end with impeachment and removal from office. They also may face prosecution, a trial, and prison time.

impeach—charge an elected official with a serious crime

Chapter 4

LEADERSHIP POSITIONS

If you like to keep other people organized, the House may have a perfect job for you. Because there are so many representatives, the House uses several leaders to keep business moving forward. It takes initiative and dedication to manage 434 other people.

The Speaker of the House is the most important leader. This role is selected by representatives of the majority party at the beginning of a new Congress. The Speaker can influence who serves on which committees, who chairs those committees, and which bills are seen by those committees.

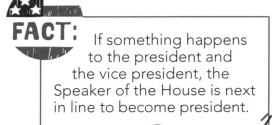

FACT: If something happens to the president and the vice president, the Speaker of the House is next in line to become president.

Paul Ryan served as the 54th Speaker of the House from 2014 to early 2019.

Committees need leadership too. The committee chairperson is usually the majority party's longest-serving member of that committee. They lead meetings and makes sure everyone follows the right rules. He or she also decides when—or whether—bills will be discussed.

The minority party's longest-serving member is called the ranking member. When political party leadership changes, the ranking member often becomes the next chairman.

About 8,000 bills are discussed in committees every year. Fewer than 10 percent of them make it to the House floor. Many bills are blocked by a chairperson or voted down by the committee. For this reason, committees are sometimes called the "graveyards of Congress."

Party leaders and whips are elected by their party's representatives. Their roles are to lead their political parties on the House floor.

After the Speaker of the House, the majority leader has the second most powerful position. He or she schedules the bills that are brought to the House floor for consideration. Planning the agenda and working to advance the goals of his or her political party are other duties. The majority whip helps the majority leader. The whip's main role is counting votes and deciding whether a bill has a chance of being passed.

Kevin McCarthy served as the House majority leader from 2014 to 2019. He became the House minority leader in 2019.

The minority leader tries to advance the goals of the **minority party**, works with the majority party and the president, and leads debate for the minority party. He or she gets help from the minority whip.

WHAT'S A WHIP?

The majority and minority whips keep track of votes for and against bills, and they try to "whip up" support among members of their parties. The word *whip* is a fox-hunting term. The "whipper-in" is the person on a fox-hunting team responsible for keeping the dogs from straying during a chase.

Representative Nancy Pelosi from California was selected as the first female minority whip in 2002. She became the first female Speaker of the House from 2007 until 2011 and was re-elected in 2019.

minority party—the party whose members make up less than half of the total membership of the group

Chapter 5

GET INVOLVED NOW!

Do you think you might want to run for a political office when you get older? It's never too early to get started!

Start by reading local and national political news stories. What is happening in these stories that interests you? Are there specific politicians you like? Study their positions on issues and figure out where you agree and disagree.

There are many other ways you can get involved:

✓ attend local rallies when politicians are present

✓ visit your representative in his or her local office

✓ go to local city council or school board meetings to watch the political process in action

✓ learn about issues that are important to your community

✓ volunteer with a parent or another older family member to collect signatures or work on an election campaign

✓ take advantage of any opportunities to be a leader in your classroom

✓ run for student government when given the chance

Representatives Alexandria Ocasio-Cortez, Barbara Lee, Annie Kuster, and Jen Schakowsky took a selfie before the 116th Congress began in 2019.

✔ learn about the details of important issues to figure out which ones you feel most strongly about

✔ talk with people who have different opinions than your own

✔ talk with family members to get their opinions about important issues, and then share yours

Speaker Nancy Pelosi (center, front row in white) with the women of the 116th Congress in front of the U.S. Capitol Building.

Historically men have taken on roles in politics. But women are catching up! In 1917 Jeannette Rankin from Montana was the first woman elected to Congress. Since then, 332 women have served as representatives, delegates, or senators. On November 6, 2018, 35 new female members were elected. They joined 65 female incumbents. This was the most diverse incoming group by race or gender in the history of the House.

2018 ELECTION FIRSTS

Ilhan Omar (1981–)

In 2018 Somali American Ilhan Omar from Minnesota and Palestinian American Rashida Tlaib from Michigan became the first Muslim women elected to Congress.

Sharice Davids from Kansas and Deb Haaland from New Mexico became the first Native American congresswomen. Davids is a member of the Ho-Chunk Nation and Haaland is an enrolled member of the Pueblo of Laguna.

Jahana Hayes from Connecticut and Ayanna Pressley from Massachusetts became the first African American women to represent New England.

At 29 years old, New York's Alexandria Ocasio-Cortez became the youngest congresswoman ever.

GLOSSARY

administration (ad-MIN-uh-stray-shuhn)—the period of time during which a government holds office

appropriations (uh-PRO-pree-ay-shuhns)—the congressional power to collect taxes and authorize spending federal government money

bipartisan (bye-PAR-tuh-suhn)—the cooperation between two political parties who usually oppose each other's policies

constituents (kuhn-STITCH-oo-uhnts)—the people who live and vote in a Congress member's home state or district

executive branch (ig-ZE-kyuh-tiv BRANCH)—the part of government that makes sure the laws are obeyed

impeach (im-PEECH)—charge an elected official with a serious crime; it can result in removal from office

incumbent (in-KUM-buhnt)—an official currently holding office

judicial branch (joo-DISH-uhl BRANCH)—the part of government that explains laws

legislative branch (LEJ-iss-lay-tiv BRANCH)—the part of government that passes bills that become laws

majority party (muh-JOR-uh-tee PAR-tee)—the party whose members make up more than half of the total membership of the group

minority party (MI-noh-ruh-tee PAR-tee)—the party whose members make up less than half of the total membership of the group

minutes (MIN-uhts)—written notes that tell what took place at a meeting

unanimous (yoo-NAN-uh-muhss)—agreed on by everyone

READ MORE

Bowers, Matt. *Understanding How Laws Are Made: American Government.* Mankato, MN: Amicus, 2020.

Burgan, Michael. *The Department of Justice: A Look Behind the Scenes.* North Mankato, MN: Compass Point Books, 2019.

Sobel, Syl. *How the U.S. Government Works, Third Edition.* Hauppauge, NY: B.E.S. Pub. Co., 2019.

INTERNET SITES

Ben's Guide to the U.S. Government
https://bensguide.gpo.gov/j-history

Scholastic News Kids Press Corps
kpcnotebook.scholastic.com

Time for Kids
www.timeforkids.com

CRITICAL THINKING QUESTIONS

1. Name the three branches of government. Describe the primary responsibility of each. Where do representatives fit in?
2. Research a bill introduced by a representative from your state. Explain what the bill does, and who it is designed to help.
3. Which leadership position sounds the most interesting to you? What appeals to you about it?

INDEX